Beautifully Quilted

with Alex Anderson

- How to Choose or Create the Best Designs for Your Quilt

- Full-size Patterns, Ready to Use

- 5 Timeless Projects

C&T PUBLISHING INC.

© 2003 Alex Anderson
Editor-in-Chief: Darra Williamson
Editor: Liz Aneloski
Technical Editor: Carolyn Aune
Copy Editor: Gael Betts
Proofreader: Eva Simoni Erb
Cover Designer: Kris Yenche
Book Designer: Staci Harpole
Design Director: Diane Pedersen
Illustrator: Kirstie McCormick
Production Assistants: Kristy A. Konitzer/Luke Mulks
Quilt Photography: Sharon Risedorph, unless otherwise noted
Instructional Photography: Diane Pedersen
Cover Photography: John Bagley and Richard Tauber
Cover Styling: John Vitale
Published by C&T Publishing, Inc., P.O. Box 1456, Lafayette,
California 94549

Anderson, Alex
 Beautifully quilted with Alex Anderson : how to choose or create the
best designs for your quilt : 5 timeless projects, full-size patterns,
ready to use.
    p. cm.
 ISBN 1-57120-190-4 (paper trade)
 1. Quilting--Design. 2. Quilting--Patterns. 3. Patchwork--Patterns.
I. Title.
 TT835 .A51693 2003
 746.46'041--dc21

                2002015798

Printed in China
10 9 8 7 6 5 4 3 2 1

Contents◆

Dedication

This book is dedicated to those who love and appreciate quilting. I hope this book inspires confidence in those wanting to master the fine art of quilt marking.

Acknowledgments

Thank you to all who helped make this book possible. Thank you to Gloria Smith and Paula Reid, whose friendship and machine quilting are a god send, and to Elke Torgersen for once again rescuing me with her beautiful handquilting, Benartex for beautiful fabric, Julie Silber for lending great photos of antique quilts, In-between Stitches in Livermore, CA for letting us invade their store for the cover photo, Lucy Hilty who opened the entire world of quilt marking to me many, many years ago, and last but not least my family, who support and help me continue this fabulous journey.

Introduction

Ever get stumped or wonder which way to turn when it's time to choose quilting designs for your pieced or appliquéd quilt? In this book you will discover the tricks and techniques for choosing appropriate quilting designs for your quilt tops and how to create your own unique designs.

Bitten hard by the quilting bug over twenty years ago, my first love with this entire process was hand quilting and watching the texture and beauty of the quilting design spring forth. My first quilt was a Grandmother's Flower Garden that my grandma started in the 1930s and I finished in the 1970s. What was intended to be a queen-size quilt ended up the size of a bath mat. Despite all of the $1/4$" quilting lines around the many tiny hexagons and the large quilting stitches, I was drawn into the hand quilting process. Off to quilt shops and quilt shows I ventured. Attending a quilt show, I hit the jackpot and purchased a twin-size sailboat quilt top that needed to be finished. I quickly snapped it up and promptly went home and put it on the frame to quilt. Half-way through, I realized there had to be more to quilting than straight lines and quilting $1/4$" from the seam allowance. How much more interesting this quilt would have been if I had explored the endless quilting design possibilities available. A little thought would have gone a long way.

Sensing that something was missing from my quilting knowledge, I took an excellent quilt-marking class from famous Mennonite quilter Lucy Hilty. She was ranked among the very best quilters in the country and opened many students' eyes to the numerous possibilities of how to create quilting designs. Sadly, she is no longer with us, but her passion and excellence in quilt marking has been passed to many fortunate students. She taught us how to draw feathers, cables, and eight-pointed stars. In addition, she taught us how to have a discerning eye when working with pre-made quilting design patterns. She unlocked the mystery of mastering quilting designs and passed the golden key to me. Interestingly, the basic design lessons I learned from traditional quilt designs apply to all quilts, both traditional and innovative.

I encourage you to become confident enough to pick up a pencil and draw, using this book as a tool. There is absolutely nothing to be intimidated by. If you can connect the dots, you can create your own quilting designs. We will start with feathers and cables and eight-pointed stars (just as I did), and I will share some neat ideas that will enable you to design your own patterns. Quilt marking and designing is just as much fun as creating the top itself. It is simply a matter of understanding the tricks and the rules.

Look how much more interesting this simple wallhanging becomes with quilted dolphins, stars, and rope.

Machine quilted by Paula Reid.
Full quilt shown on page 46.

Tools·and·Terms

TOOLS

The following tools have become staples for drawing quilting designs. Many of these tools are available at your local quilt shop or fabric store. If not, check out your local art or drafting supply store. Stored with care, they will last you a lifetime.

Pencil, Sharpener, and Eraser

It all starts here. Any pencil will do (mechanical or standard). You just need one with a nice sharp tip (an electric or battery sharpener is very nice to keep handy). Don't be afraid of the pencil. It will soon become your best friend. Remember that it has two ends: the lead and the eraser. Always keep in mind that no design is set in stone until the stitches are laid in place, and even then, changes are possible.

Paper Scissors and Rotary Cutter

A good pair of sharp paper scissors is handy to have. The rotary cutter I use for paper has an old blade that is less-than-perfect for fabric. Both are marked with a tied ribbon to distinguish them from my fabric scissors and rotary cutter.

Black Permanent Felt-Tip Pen

I purchase these by the box. After the quilting designs are established, I go over the pencil lines with the Sharpie fine-point permanent pen (not the fineliner).

Paper

There are many different types of paper available that will work quite well, each offering its own benefits and limitations.

◆ **17" x 22" Graph Paper (4 or 8 grids per inch)**
Graph paper is typically available by individual sheet and by the pad. It is more economical to purchase a pad. The light grid lines make drawing the pattern within the desired space very easy. In addition, the grid increments are helpful to keep the pattern evenly spaced when dividing up the areas of the quilt to be quilted. When the space you are designing for is larger than the sheet of paper, tape the appropriate number of sheets of paper together with clear tape. In addition, gridded paper is resistant to multiple erasures.

◆ **Velum on a Roll**
Velum is a heavy-duty tracing paper. It is translucent, yet strong enough to withstand multiple erasures. This is a nice feature when you are faced with drafting patterns. It comes in varying widths on a roll (18" or wider). Velum is expensive, so look to your pocketbook and purchase the widest roll you can afford.

◆ **Tracing Paper on a Roll**
Tracing paper is much less expensive than velum and is also translucent. However, it is not as sturdy as velum and will not hold up to multiple erasures. Again, look to your pocket book and purchase the widest roll you can afford.

◆ White Butcher Paper on a Roll

This very economical paper is what I use for patterns. It is not translucent, but it is tough and will stand up to multiple erasures.

Most of these papers are also available by the sheet or pad. If necessary, you can purchase extra-large tablets of the paper you want to work with. The advantages of a roll of paper are that you can easily draw borders, and purchasing by the roll is more economical. In all cases, if the design you are working on exceeds the size of the paper, you can piece it together with clear tape.

Rulers

Although any ruler will work, I like to use a 2" x 18" see-through drafting ruler. In addition, a yardstick comes in handy for longer lines.

Compass

This handy tool comes in a variety of styles, prices, and quality. The kind of compass used in grade school is perfectly fine for small to medium circles. The only problem is that sometimes they slip and refuse to hold true to a size. A more expensive compass is nice to work with and will hold the size. Make sure it comes with an extesion arm for drawing larger circles. For really large circles, there is a tool made especially for yardsticks. This gives you the ability to draw circles up to 72"!

Protractor

Any protractor will work quite nicely. It is important that you understand exactly where the 0° line is: some protractors have it on the edge, and some have it set in $1/4$" or so.

Light Table

A light table provides a light source that will enable you to trace your paper pattern onto the quilt top. Any flat, clear surface with light shining through will work. It can be as simple as a window. My light table is an 18" x 36" piece of $1/4$"-thick, clear Plexiglas. When it is time to draw, I set it between two chairs and put a lamp under it. If you have a dining room table that extends with leaves, consider getting the Plexiglas cut a couple inches larger than the size of your leaves. Extend your table but do not put the leaves in. Place the Plexiglas over the opening and place a lamp under it. Your table will surround the "light box." Of course, a commercial light box will also work, but I prefer having a larger surface to work on.

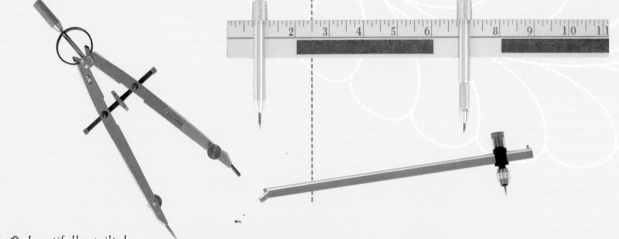

Marking Tools

I am frequently asked, "What do you mark with?" After I gracefully try to dodge the question (because there is no definitive answer), my answer usually is a Silver Verithin pencil. For additions and corrections while quilting, I use a white charcoal pencil or white chalk powder. If none of these work and you need to introduce a color, always test to make sure the mark will come out. Sometimes the color in the marking tools reacts with the finish on the cloth and refuses to come off, resulting in permanent marks. Always read the instructions that come with the different products. Avoid using a #2 lead pencil. The lead is soft and thick and cannot be easily removed. To avoid making any markings, $^1/_4$"-wide quilting masking tape is a wonderful option for straight-line grids.

TERMS

Quilters have a language that is unique to the process. The following terms, phrases, and words relate directly to quilting designs. Become familiar with them.

◆ $^1/_4$" quilting: Stitch $^1/_4$" from the sewn seam. This technique allows you to stitch through multiple layers of seam allowances. It is commonly used by beginners. (See page 9.)

◆ Quilting in the ditch: Stitch directly next to the sewn or appliquéd seam, on the side of the seam without the seam allowance.

◆ Echo quilting: Evenly space the lines of quilting beginning directly next to the sewn or appliquéd seam and repeating outward to fill in the background, kind of like ripples that happen when you throw a pebble into a calm lake.

◆ Stipple quilting: Stitch closely spaced, continuous squiggley lines that never cross over each other to fill in the background. (See page 9.)

Choosing · Quilting · Designs

Traditional and innovative quilts have several things in common when you are considering which quilting designs to use. The guidelines generally hold true for both, and are also applicable to both machine and hand quilting. When I am deciding how to quilt my tops, I always keep the guidelines in mind. However, as we all know, guidelines are subject to interpretation. Each quilt top needs to be considered individually. This makes the entire quilting journey an interesting and challenging experience from conception to conclusion.

GUIDELINES

◆ Will intricate quilting designs show? Not all quilts are candidates for awesome quilting designs. It is a sad day when you have spent the time stitching incredible quilted motifs only to find that they are lost in the pattern of the fabric. If a quilt is destined for fabulous quilting, make sure that the fabric you use is plain enough to let the quilting designs show. While planning the quilt, designate areas that will be highlighted with quilting. Solid-colored fabrics are your best bet for those areas, or a printed fabric that reads almost as a solid will work. If you are at all unsure, test the quilting on the fabric to see if it shows.

If your border fabric is highly patterned and fancy quilting isn't going to show, I have two solutions that work quite well.

1 Follow the printed fabric design to create your quilting design. When using this technique, make sure that there is an even density of quilting.

2 Fans and cables are another nice solution. They are repetitive, so the brain can easily identify what the pattern is.

Fans

Cable

Fan design on printed fabric

Sometimes just by changing the thread color used for quilting, the design will become more prominent.

Quilting with white thread

Quilting with pink thread

◆ Many times new quilters are taught to quilt ¼" from the sewn line. I believe this is so the quilter does not have to decide what to quilt and can simply get her hands going. The problem is that this technique can lead to some areas being heavily quilted while other areas are left without enough quilting.

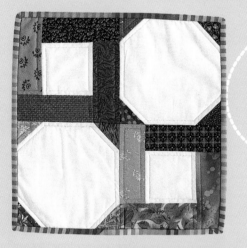

¼" quilting

◆ Fill the space. Remember when you were in kindergarten and your teacher would constantly remind you to fill the space? The same holds true when deciding what designs to quilt. A design that is too small looks awkward and empty. If you are filling a specific area, for example an alternate solid-color block, end the design about ¼" from the sewn line. In addition to filling the space, this will help avoid quilting through the seam allowances.

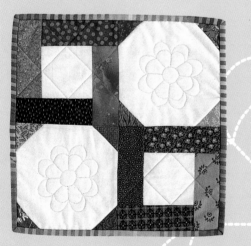

Not adequately filling the space

◆ Use an equal amount of quilting over the entire surface. If one area is tightly quilted and another area is left empty, not only will the quilt look odd, but it will not lie flat or hang straight.

Uneven amount of quilting

◆ Be careful not to over quilt, especially when machine quilting. The quilt might become stiff.

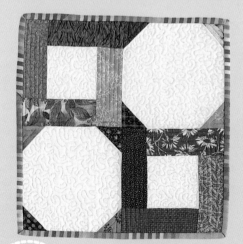

Too much quilting

◆ Use an adequate amount of quilting. Even the simplest quilt deserves due respect. Always read the batting manufacturer's recommended quilting density for the specific batting you are working with. Also follow the manufacturer's instructions for proper preparation for use.

Adequate amount of quilting

◆ It's okay, and in fact perfectly fine, to cross over seam lines of pieced units. Look how much more interesting it is to have a crosshatch grid crossing over pieced seamlines than ¹/₄" quilting would have been. Also, a border consisting of several units (inner borders and a main border) can be quilted with one motif. This gives you more area to create in. This is also true for sashing and divider strips as shown in Gloria Smith's quilt below.

Meghan's Quilt
Machine pieced and machine quilted by Gloria Smith.

◆ It is nice to mix geometric lines with soft, curved lines. That is why you will often see gridded backgrounds used with fancy motifs. They work well together and act as complements. The gridded background accentuates the fancy designs. Make sure the density of the grid is in proportion to the size and scale of the design.

Motif with no background quilting

Motif with grid quilting

◆ Before you start to design your quilting designs you must determine if your quilt is going to be quilted by hand or by machine. If you are designing for hand quilting, anything goes. If machine work is in the quilt's future, consider how many stop/starts you are creating. For example, a cable (page 44) would be an excellent option for machine quilting, while grapes (page 32) should probably be avoided. A little forethought will help avoid frustration at the machine.

COMMERCIAL TEMPLATES

There are thousands of commercial templates available on the market today. It is important to be able to assess the quality of the template. Just because a template is stamped in plastic or printed in a book does not mean it is good quality. Is the design appealing? Do the lines flow? Is it balanced? Look at the illustration below. Notice how the top feathers flow gracefully from the center stem. However, the bottom half does not flow smoothly from the center stem. I have seen both types of wreaths side by side in the same publication. Become a critic when you assess pre-existing patterns.

Top = Design flows gracefully from center stem.
Bottom = Design does not flow gracefully from center stem.

It is very easy to customize templates and patterns. By making simple changes or corrections, you can take a pattern and make it your own. A really neat trick is to take an existing pattern, trace it on a piece of paper and then either add or delete lines. Look how this simple cable takes on a new look by adding and subtracting lines.

Original double cable design

Overlapping lines added to double cable

Motif added to triple cable

Feather replacing half of triple cable

The copy machine can help you adjust a template design to the correct size. Trace the template pattern onto a piece of paper and simply reduce or enlarge it to the correct size. Remember to fill the space up to $1/4$" from the pieced line.

DESIGN TRANSFER

Once you are satisfied with the quilting design, it is time to transfer it onto the quilt top. If you are working on a light fabric, the pencil lines drawn on the paper might be dark enough. If not, re-mark the pattern on the paper with a permanent felt-tip pen. Chances are your drawings will be on several different pieces of paper. Pin one section to the underneath side of the quilt top, avoiding pinning where the drawn lines are. Mark the section. Remove the paper template before starting on the next section. Mark the entire quilt before you baste it. Mark it dark enough so you can see the lines, but light enough for easy removal. If you will be working in a hoop, the quilt will need to be marked darker than if you will be working on a quilting frame, since the hoop will rub the lines off more quickly than working on a frame will.

IDEAS

Inspiration comes from everywhere. The most obvious place is other quilts! Whenever I go to quilt shows, I look very carefully at how the quiltmaker handled the situation. How did they fill the space or turn the corners? Did they use any interesting motifs I have not seen before? If I see something unique or unusual, at a minimum I take a mental note, or better yet, I quickly jot it down. There are some really great designs being created today which are worth noting.

Books are another wonderful resource. My collection of books spans the years. I am particularly drawn to books that feature antique quilts. The photos need to clearly show the quilting designs. Amish quilt books are included in my collection. I pour over the photos, taking careful note of all the wonderful ideas and inspiration they provide.

Before I built my large book collection, the public library was my hangout. My local library is rich with quilting books because before she passed away, a friend of mine requested that any gifts in her memory be contributed to the quilting section of the local library. How wonderful that she had a broad vision for the quilters of our valley.

If you have yet to join the local guild, do it! Often, they too have a substantial library for members to use. If your guild doesn't have a members' library, it's time to start one.

In college, I had a wonderful professor in Wood Shop 101. His goal was to teach us the basics about wood and furniture construction, but more importantly, he wanted us to learn how to distinguish good furniture from poorly designed and poorly constructed goods. This is my wish for you regarding quilting designs. Learn what works and why. Quilts are an excellent resource. Open your eyes and ask why this quilt is working, or why it is not. I am sure you will become as fascinated with this process as I am.

Center Diamond, courtesy of Julie Silber

Amish Bars, courtesy of Julie Silber

CONTROLLER'S DREAM
Machine pieced and hand quilted by Alex Anderson.

The graphic boldness of the pieced top coupled with soft elegant quilting provides an unusual combination. "Layers" of geometric lines and soft lines complement each other. The background grid, emphasizing the beautiful feathers topped with an eight-pointed star, gives an interesting dimension.

STARRY NIGHT
Machine pieced and hand quilted by Alex Anderson.

*A double-feathered wreath was chosen to fill the center square rather than large feathers.
The size and scale of the feathers complement the entire look of the quilt. Metallic thread
was used to give extra sparkle to the quilt.*

IT'S IN THE STARS
Machine pieced and hand quilted by Alex Anderson.

A folded-corners inner feather border adds as much dimension as a pieced inner border would provide.
Little stars in the large pieced stars add a geometric dimension to the quilt and compliment the pieced stars.

CALIFORNIA
Machine pieced and hand quilted
by Alex Anderson.

This quilt could not support intricate quilting, so the combination of a geometric grid and soft curves solved the problem. The poppies have been quilted to look like real flowers with a glisten of beading to reflect the morning dew.

TAWANDA
Machine pieced and hand quilted
by Alex Anderson.

This quilt is another example of a piece that does not support elaborate quilting. An irregular grid in the center compliments the edgy look of the quilt, and a twisted cable adds a soft touch to the checkerboard area.

Drawing ·Quilting· Designs

GENERAL TIPS

◆ Here's how to divide up space between parallel lines.

1 Draw a square the desired finished size (10" for our example). Label the sides A and B.

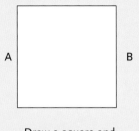

Draw a square and
label A and B.

2 Decide how many sections you want to divide your square into (4 for our example). Find a number that is divided evenly by the number of sections and is larger than the size of the square (12 divides into 4 sections evenly and is larger than the 10" square). Place the 0 end of your ruler on side A and the 12" mark on side B of the square. Divide the larger number (12") by the number of sections (4) to get the measurement to mark the sections (3"). Make marks at these increments (every 3"). If the ruler does not fit within the square, extend the B line upward.

3 Draw the grid lines, parallel to sides A and B of the square, at the marks. This method can be used to divide cables.

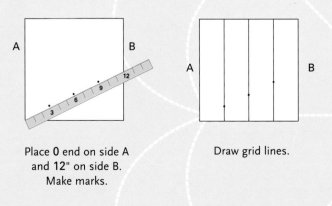

Place **0** end on side A
and 12" on side B.
Make marks.

Draw grid lines.

4 To create a grid, follow steps 1–3 above, then turn the paper one-quarter turn and mark grid lines the other direction.

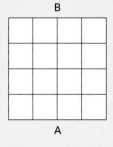

Turn paper and draw lines.

◆ Finding the center of a paper block pattern is easy. Position your ruler corner to corner and draw a short line near the center. Then, reposition your ruler from the other corner to corner and again draw a short line. This will give you an X in the center. Instead of using a ruler and pencil, you can also find the center by folding the paper in half along the diagonals.

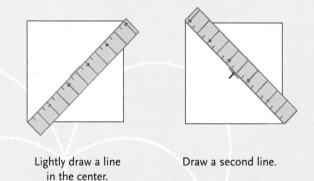

Lightly draw a line
in the center.

Draw a second line.

◆ If you are going to be drawing multiple circles using a compass, consider reinforcing the center of the paper, where the point of the compass will be resting, by placing a little piece of masking tape on the back. This will strengthen the paper when you use the compass.

◆ It is easier to draw an arc away from your body than toward yourself. It is a more natural angle for your hand and wrist.

The following two exercises are fun and easy to do. With a few simple folds and snips you can create some classic designs.

EIGHT-SECTION DESIGNS

1 Cut a square of paper the size of the design needed ($1/4$" smaller than the pieced area, to allow for the seam allowances).

2 Fold in half once, then fold in half again.

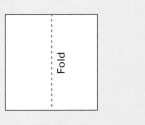

Fold in half.   Fold in half again.

3 Fold in half diagonally.

4 Draw and cut an arc on the large end of the shape.

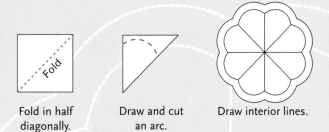

Fold in half   Draw and cut   Draw interior lines.
diagonally.   an arc.

5 The options are endless. For example, open the paper and draw the interior lines $1/4$" from the outer edge of the paper, and then draw the straight lines.

Options: Cut another arc at the pointed end of the shape, or trace the cut shape onto another piece of paper and add the outer scallops.

TWELVE-SECTION DESIGNS

1 Cut a square of paper the size of the design needed ($1/4$" smaller than the pieced area, to allow for the seam allowances).

2 Fold in half once, then fold in half again.

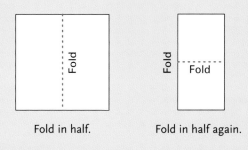

Fold in half.   Fold in half again.

3 Fold in thirds to create three triangle shapes.

4 Draw and cut an arc on the large end of the shape.

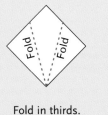

Fold in thirds.   Draw and cut
                          an arc.

Option: Before you open and draw, consider cutting another arc at the pointed end of the shape. It is amazing how easy it is to create designs simply by trying different ideas. Open the paper and draw the interior lines.

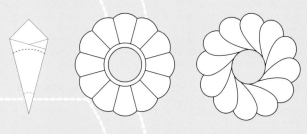

It's simple to create!

The following quilting designs can be used on the contemporary diamond quilt (page 44). It is so much fun to mix the old quilting patterns with fresh, updated colors. I love to mix the old with the new.

EIGHT-POINTED STAR

This star is found in the center of many Amish quilts. As a pieced block, its common name is the Lemoyne Star. The following star will fit quite nicely inside the 18" feathered wreath on the diamond wallhanging (page 44).

1 Draw a 6" square.

2 Place a ruler, or fold the paper, corner to corner in both directions and mark the center.

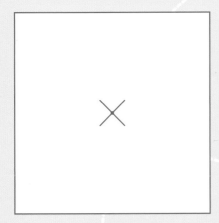

Mark center.

3 Place the point of your compass on one corner of the square and open the compass until the pencil reaches the center of the square.

4 Keeping the compass point on the corner of the square, swing the pencil end in both directions, to mark an arc on each adjacent side.

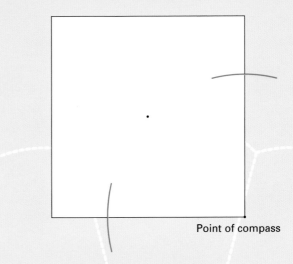

Point of compass

Mark an arc on each side.

5 Repeat on all four corners. You will end up with two marks on each side of the square. Mark a dot where each arc crosses the side of the square.

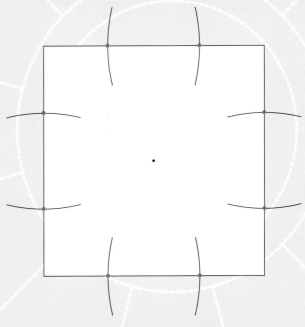

Make two marks from each corner.

6 Label the dots A-H

7 Draw lines to connect A-F, B–E, H-C, G-D and then A-D, H-E, C-F, B-G.

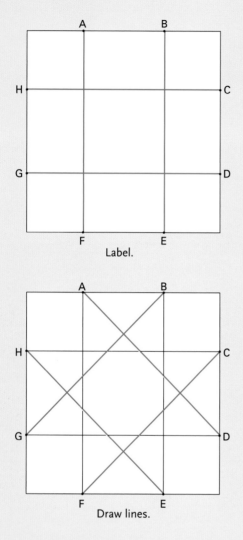

Label.

Draw lines.

8 Erase all of the interior lines.

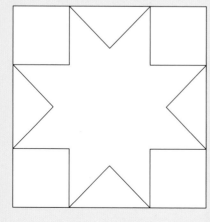

Erase interior lines.

9 Draw lines connecting each inside corner to the inside corner directly across from it.

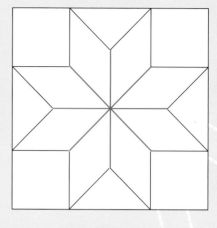

Add interior lines.

10 Using your ruler, add lines ¹/₄" outside the star lines.

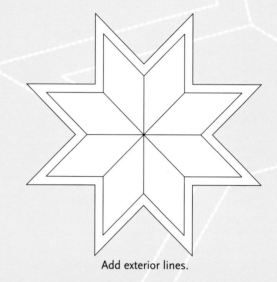

Add exterior lines.

To draw a star within any size wreath, draw a square that will fit within the inner circle of the wreath. Draw the star and add lines ¹/₄" outside the star lines to fill in the wreath's center.

CABLE

Cables are really quite simple. This cable will fit on the bar quilt. (See page 42.)

1 Draw a 3¹⁄₂" x 10¹⁄₂" rectangle.

2 Divide the 10¹⁄₂" rectangle into three units 3¹⁄₂" x 3¹⁄₂".

3 Find the center of each unit by lightly drawing diagonal lines from corner to corner. Mark the centers. Now, you can erase the diagonal center lines if you want to.

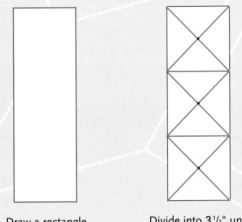

Draw a rectangle.   Divide into 3¹⁄₂" units and mark centers.

4 Set your compass at 1¹⁄₂". Place the point on the center of each square and draw a circle.

5 In each circle, draw a cat eye about 1" x ¹⁄₂". Note how they are positioned. Make sure the arcs of your cat eye are nice and smooth.

Draw circles and cat eyes.

6 Add dots and number as shown.

7 Draw lines connecting 1 to 2, 3 to 4, 5 to 6, and 7 to 8. The lines should be parallel. Erase the numbers.

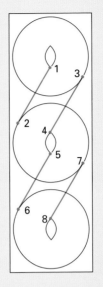

Number and draw lines.

8 Number the under twist of the cable 1–8 as shown. Draw lines from 1 to 2, 3 to 4, 5 to 6, and 7 to 8. Draw only the solid lines. The dotted lines indicate where the line "goes under" the other line. Erase the numbers.

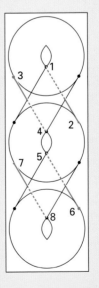

Number and draw lines.

9 Erase all unnecessary guide lines.

Erase guide lines.

10 Using the technique on page 17 divide the cable into equal sections.

Divided cable

It's as easy as that! Now with a few extra lines drawn and erased here and there, you can customize your cable in no time.

> *For cables of other sizes, cut your paper to fill the space and divide into sections (either by measuring or folding) as close to square as possible. The drawing procedure is the same.*

Sometimes you cannot divide the space evenly. It's okay to put spaces between the squares to elongate the cable. It's also okay to overlap the circles, which will give you full, chubby cable.

FEATHERED WREATH

I love feather quilting designs. They really are not difficult to create. The manipulations and variations of feathers are endless. The following exercise is for a classic 18" double-sided feather wreath. I like feathered wreaths with a double center spine. Once you become comfortable with feathers you will no longer need to segment the spaces with your protractor, but for beginners it makes the task of drawing feathers simpler.

Interior Markings

1 Draw an 18" square. Place a ruler, or fold the paper, corner to corner in both directions and mark the center.

18"

Mark center.

2 Reinforce the center with a piece of masking tape on the wrong side.

3 Using a compass, draw four circles: 17" (open compass to 8½"), 13" (open compass to 6½"), 12½" (open compass to 6¼"), 8½" (open compass to 4¼"). Note that with this classic feathered wreath, the inside ring is the same width (2") as the outer ring.

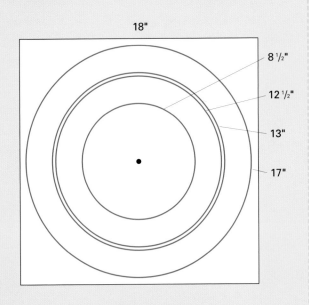

Draw four circles.

Outer Ring Feathers

4 Place the protractor with the 0° base line exactly on the center of the ring and make marks every 10° on half of the circle.

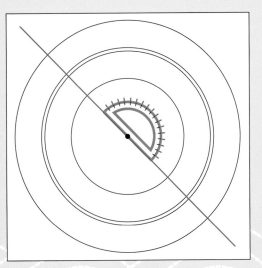

Mark every 10°.

5 In the outer ring only, lightly mark the 10° sections around the circle.

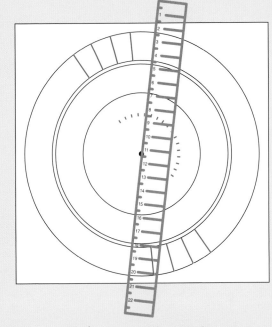

Mark 10° sections in outer ring.

6 Draw arcs from line to line around the outer ring. Make sure they are nice and round, not lopsided or pointy. It's okay if they extend a little outside the ring.

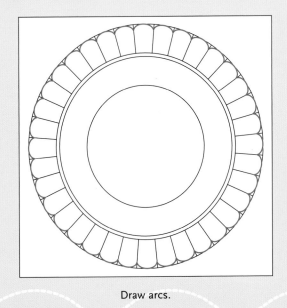

Draw arcs.

HINT: You can use a coin to help you draw the arcs. Or, when you have an arc shape you like, trace it and use it as a pattern for the rest of the arcs.

7 Draw a feather in each section, crossing over into the neighboring section at the pointed end. The drawn circles and segments are merely guides. It's okay to draw the design lines across the circle and segment lines if your feathers need a little shaping up.

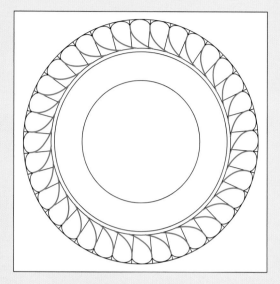

Draw a feather in each section.

Completed Outer Feathers

Inner Ring Feathers

One major misconception is that there need to be as many feathers in the inner ring as in the outer ring. In fact, there will be fewer. If you have as many feathers in the inner as the outer, the inner feathers will be scrunched and bunched. Also, they do not need to line up in any specific format. Each feather is its own independent marcher that stands on its own. The goal is to have the inner and outer feathers appear to be the same size.

Too many inner ring feathers

Proper number of inner ring feathers

8 Place the protractor 0° base line exactly on the center of the ring and mark every 15°, the same way you marked the 10° markings.

NOTE: These 15° divisions will not line up with the 10° divisions.

9 In the inner ring only, lightly mark the 15° sections.

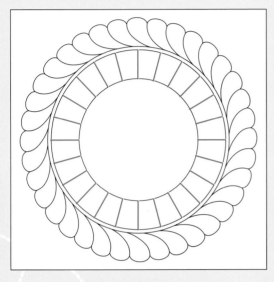

Mark 15° sections.

10 Draw arcs from line to line around the inside edge. Make sure they are nice and round, not lopsided or pointy.

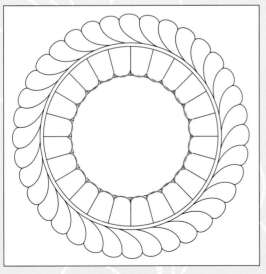

Draw arcs.

11 Draw a feather in each 15° section, crossing over into the neighboring section at the pointed end. The drawn arcs and segments are merely guides. It's okay to draw the design lines across the circle and segment lines if your feathers need a little shaping up.

Draw a feather in each section.

12 Complete the wreath.

Completed Wreath

Many people find the inner feathers easier to draw because the arc of the inner circle provides a natural curve.

Time for feather assessment:
The goal is to create perfect feathers that flow comfortably from the center line.

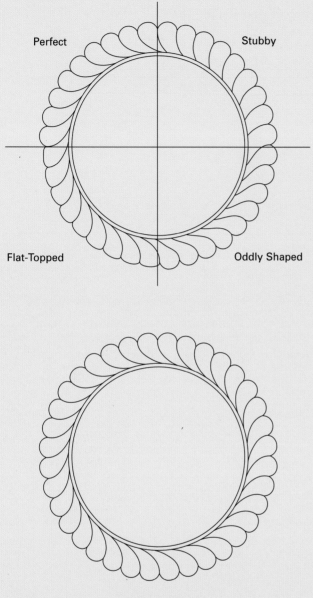

Perfect   Stubby

Flat-Topped   Oddly Shaped

Perfect Feathers

Not all feathers work out the first time. In fact, they take a little practice. Look closely and ask yourself, "Do my feathers flow gracefully from the spine?"

Once you gain confidence with feathers, they are easy to draw without the aid of a protractor. Draw several arcs around the edge of the circle and then fill in the feathers. The key is to keep the arcs consistent in size. A coin can come in handy: a dime is a good size for miniatures and a half dollar works well for large wreaths. Once you become comfortable drawing wreaths, the size of the feathers becomes second nature.

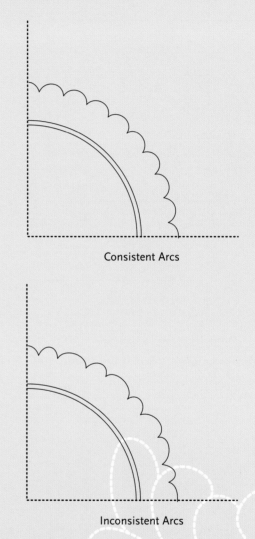

Consistent Arcs

Inconsistent Arcs

When drawing feather designs of varying sizes, just remember to keep them an appealing size and density. Feathers can be drawn with numerous manipulations. Now it's your turn to draw, experiment, and play.

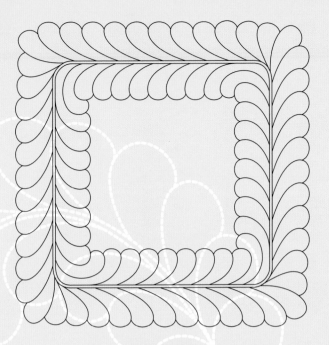

Wreath Variation

Meandering Feather

BORDER OR SASHING CORNERS

There are many ways to turn a corner with a quilting design. Some are more pleasing than others.

Example 1: Run the design off the edge. This decision may be used on a folk art style of quilt. It gives an easy, casual look.

Run design off edge.

Example 2: Use a simple motif in the corner. If you want to have a more controlled look, this is an easy solution.

Use simple motif.

Example 3: My favorite choice for elegance is to gracefully turn the corner.

Gracefully turn corner.

Turned-Feather Corner

These are elegant motifs. While they look complicated, they are very simple to create once you understand how to draw a basic feather.

1 Cut a piece of paper 6" x 15". This 15" section is half of the 6"-wide border length, starting at the corner.

2 At one end, mark a 45° line to make a 6" triangle.

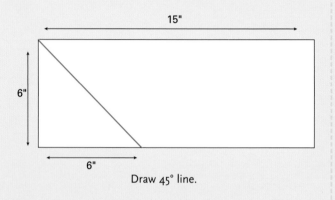

Draw 45° line.

3 Draw parallel lines along the two sides, 1 1/2" from each long edge.

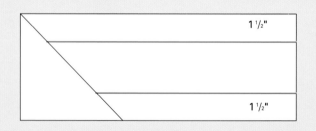

Draw parallel lines.

4 Using these two lines as guides, draw an S-curve with two lines 3/8" apart, for the center spine.

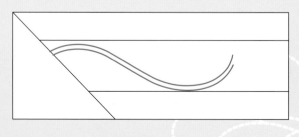

Draw center spine.

5 Draw a line parallel to each side of the S-curve, 1 3/8" from the spine.

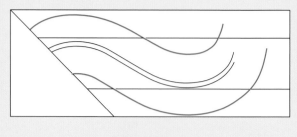

Draw lines.

6 Starting at the center, draw the top half of a heart in each section. You can use a quarter to help draw the arc.

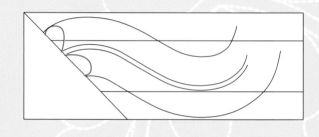

Draw half heart.

7 Draw the feather arcs along each edge line. Remember to keep them balanced and uniform in size.

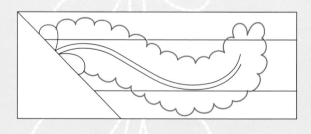

Draw feather arcs.

8 Fill in the feathers.

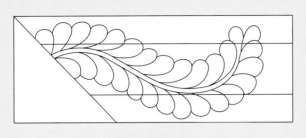

Fill in feathers.

9 Flop the design to turn the corner.

Flop the design.

TIP: For extra-wide borders, consider sweeping looped spines that flow from the center spine. This creates a VERY elegant look.

Feather with looped spines flowing from center spine

Turned Cable Corner

1 Cut an L shaped piece of paper 24" x 6" x 18".

2 Divide it into 6" square increments.

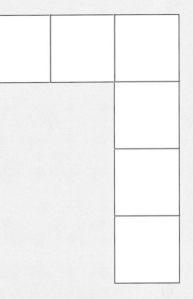

Divide into squares.

3 Lightly draw diagonal lines from corner to corner in each square to find the center. Mark the centers.

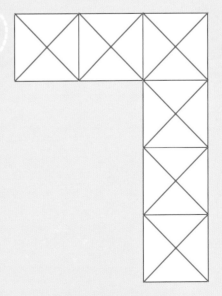

Draw lines and mark centers.

4 Erase the diagonal lines.

5 Set your compass at 2³/₄". Place the point on the center of each square and draw a 5¹/₂" circle.

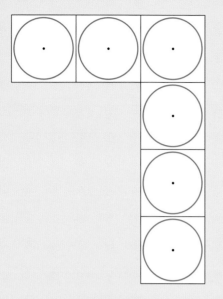

Draw circles.

6 Draw a 1¹/₂" circle at the center point of the corner square.

7 In each of the remaining squares, draw a cat eye about 1¹/₂" x ³/₄". Note how they are positioned. Make sure the top and bottom arcs of your cat eyes are smooth and even.

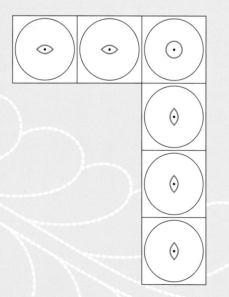

Draw center circle and cat eyes.

8 Add dots and number as shown.

9 It's time to connect the dots. Draw lines from 1 to 2, from 3 to 4, 5 to 6, 7 to 8, 9 to 10, and 11 to 12. The lines should be parallel. Erase the numbers.

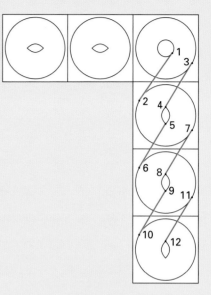

Number and draw lines.

10 Number the under twist of the cable 1–8 as shown. Draw lines from 1 to 2, 3 to 4, 5 to 6, and 7 to 8. Draw only the solid lines. Erase the numbers.

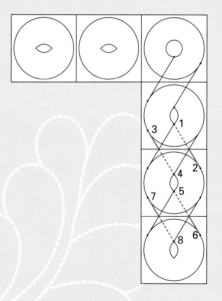

Number and draw lines.

11 Number 1–10 as shown. Draw lines from 1 to 2, 3 to 4, 5 to 6 to 7, and 8 to 9 to 10. Notice how lines 5–7 and 8–10 have a subtle curve. Erase the numbers.

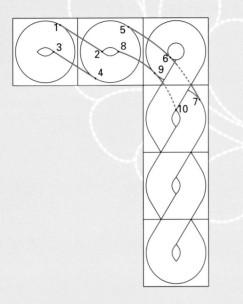

Number and draw lines.

12 Number 1–8 as shown. Draw lines from 1 to 2, 3 to 4, 5 to 6, and 7 to 8. Draw the solid lines. The dotted lines indicate where the cable "goes under." Using the technique on page 17 divide the cable into equal sections. Continue drawing additional cable sections to complete the length needed.

Number and draw lines.

Finished Turned-Corner Cable

Turned-Feather Corner Variation

If your border has an even number of segments on each side you only need to draw one corner because they will all turn the same. If your border has an odd number of increments, you will need to draw two different corners.

Repeat Motifs

It is very easy to create an interesting wreath or border working with simple motifs. For example, the holly leaf and berry is very easy to draw and when placed in an interesting arrangement, offers endless opportunities.

For a wreath, draw a circle and randomly place the holly and berries around the circle.

Holly Leaf and Berries

Holly Wreath

The border can be handled in a similar manner. Cut paper to size for one quarter of the border (including the corner). Again, arrange the holly and berries in a pleasing manner. Think of it as a flower arrangement you have prepared for your table: there isn't a right or wrong way, just the way that looks pleasing to your eye.

Holly Border

The original inspiration for the grape wreath came from an Amish quilt. Start with a circle, which turns into the vine of the wreath. Draw a few leaves in different sizes and add the grapes. I used a quarter to help draw the grapes for a this 20" wreath.

Grape Wreath

Unlikely Inspirations

This design was inspired by an antique stained glass window that hangs in my home.

I think the tulip has an interesting shape and makes a nice quilting design. Draw only half of the tulip (similar to drawing hearts), then fold the paper in half and trace the other side.

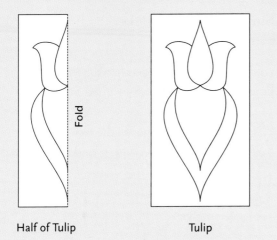

Half of Tulip

Tulip

Mark the center of the square, draw four tulips facing out toward the corners of the square in a cross pattern, then add more tulips to fill in the empty spaces. Whenever an area is left empty, consider filling it with repeated shapes.

Add more tulips.

Take time to look around you for inspiration. I pictured the front porch on my parent's home as a potential border.

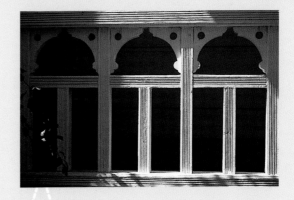

I cut the paper one quarter of the finished size, including a corner. I drew a diagonal line across the outside corner at 45 degrees as a starting point.

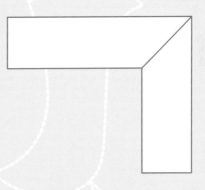

Diagonal line drawn.

It is important to evenly divide the space, which defines areas to create in.

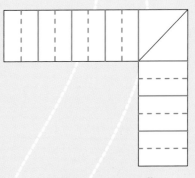

Space broken up equally.

I drew multiple arcs in each design space, which reflect the look of the porch rail. Once I liked the way the lines flowed it was easy to repeat the pattern in each designated space. I drew in half the corner, stopping at the diagonal line, folded the paper and traced the other side. The design automatically turned the corner.

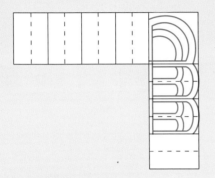

Multiple arcs and half of corner drawn.

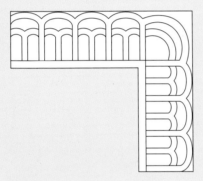

Completed Design

Starting from Scratch

The following technique is very freeing and allows you to make random decisions as you go. Here is how I came up with this original design.

First, I cut a piece of paper the exact size of the area that needed to be filled with a quilting design.

Cut paper the size of the space.

I marked the center and used my compass to draw two circles in the center.

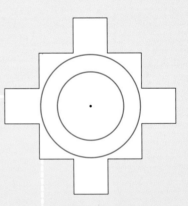

Draw two circles in the center.

I divided the shape into eight wedge-shaped sections.

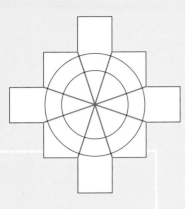

Divide into sections.

Starting in the center section, I drew a leaf shape. It didn't seem to have enough lines, so I drew in another leaf. To fill the unused space, I drew feathers.

Draw design lines.

I repeated the leaf and feather motif in all the sections. There it is—an original design. It might seem a little overwhelming at first, but it was only a matter of breaking the area into sections and taking it one step at a time.

Repeat in all sections.

Working with a Simple Shape

There are basic shapes we use day in and day out that we must not overlook for quilting designs: stars, rectangles, squares, circles, handprints, cookie cutter shapes, and even baby's handprints.

Quilted Baby Handprint

Let's look at the possibilities that a circle offers. You can make circles using your protractor, the base of a glass, or even a circle cut from a square of paper. Each offers different sizes and possibilities.

Circles were overlapped in a grid.
Double lines were then added in the center of each circle.
Lines were erased where the circles overlapped.

With a few lines removed it becomes a pumpkin seed design.

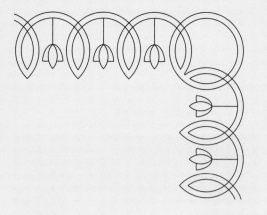

REPEAT DESIGNS

If you are really stumped when picking a quilting design that is appropriate for your quilt, here is a trick that works quite well. Look to the pieced or appliquéd shapes and repeat them. The border on this quilt is spectacular, adding to the glory of the entire piece. Gloria used thread colors to re-create the look of the pieced units in the blocks. In essence, the quilting mimics the pieced border shapes, sewn in multiple rows of colorful thread.

This border was also created by overlapping double circles. The empty space was then filled with a simple tulip.

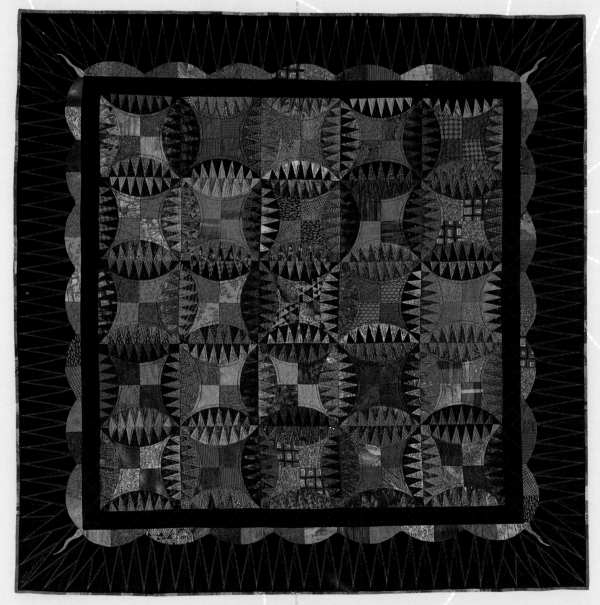

Dancing in the Moonlight
Machine pieced and quilted by Gloria Smith.

As mentioned in the beginning of the book, not all quilts are destined for fabulous quilting designs. The effort and work can become lost in the piecing and fabric prints of some quilts. I have come up with a few ideas on how to handle these situations. Basically, combine soft curves and geometric grids to cover the entire surface. Just as in traditional quilt design, they complement each other. Use equal amounts of quilting over the entire surface. If you decide to use soft curved lines in the body of the quilt, a geometric grid will work quite well on the border. If you decide to use a geometric grid in the center of the quilt, soft curved lines will work best on the border. For soft and curving borders I look to fans and cables as my first choice.

HOW TO DRAW SOFT, CURVED LINES

Picture an organic shape and how it softly flows from one unit to another. Keep that image in mind as you approach this.

1 Divide your quilt into two sections: the border and the center. For the center, draw a few lines across the surface of the quilt. Have them flow gracefully from either the edge or from each other. Keep the curves open and flowing. Keep the curves larger than 90°.

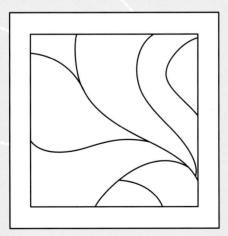

Draw soft curved lines.

2 Draw echo quilting lines about 1" apart using the main curving lines as your guide. This is an excellent pattern for machine quilting.

Draw echo quilting lines.

3 When you are satisfied with the center, consider using a geometric grid in the border. The two styles of lines (soft vs. geometric) work well together.

Echo quilting with grid in border

Angel Quilt
Machine pieced, hand appliquéd, and hand quilted by Alex Anderson and, embroidered by Estella Gonzales.

I used an overall, soft-curved quilting design. The border offered the perfect opportunity to use a geometric grid.

GRID QUILTING DESIGNS

Geometric grids also work well on even the most complicated quilt.

Unusual grids are also fun to use. It is simply a matter of auditioning and experimenting until you find just the right look for your quilt.

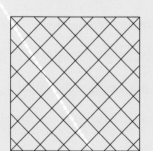
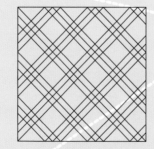
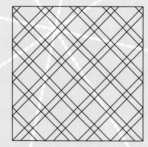
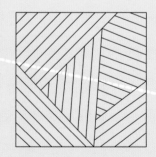

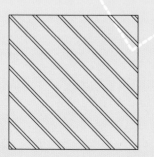

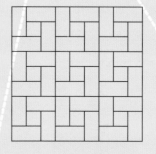
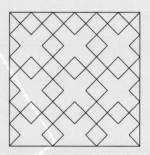

Pinwheels and Feathers

This quilt is 56½" x 56½" and is made of twenty-five 6" Nine-Patch Pinwheel blocks and twenty-four 6" large alternate blocks. Pieced and hand quilted by Alex Anderson.

FABRIC REQUIREMENTS

Fabric amounts are based on a 42" fabric width.

Off-white: $3^3/_4$ yards for Pinwheel background, small and large alternate blocks, border #2, and triangles in border #3

Assorted Batiks: $3/_4$ yard total for Pinwheel blocks

Gold Batik: $3/_8$ yard for triangles in border #3

Print: $1/_4$ yard for border #1

Backing: $3^1/_2$ yards

Batting: 61" x 61"

Binding: $1/_2$ yard

CUTTING

Off-white

◆ Cut 2 lengthwise strips (parallel to the selvage) $5^3/_4$" x 44" for the top and bottom borders #2.

◆ Cut 2 lengthwise strips $5^3/_4$" x $54^1/_2$" for the side borders #2.

◆ Cut 4 strips $6^1/_2$" x fabric width, then cut into 24 squares $6^1/_2$" x $6^1/_2$" for large alternate blocks.

◆ Cut 12 strips $1^7/_8$" x fabric width, then cut into 250 squares $1^7/_8$" x $1^7/_8$", then cut in half diagonally for pinwheels.

◆ Cut 7 strips $2^1/_2$" x fabric width, then cut into 100 squares $2^1/_2$" x $2^1/_2$" for the small alternate blocks.

◆ Cut 3 strips $3^1/_4$" x fabric width, then cut into 27 squares $3^1/_4$" x $3^1/_4$", then cut in half diagonally twice for border #3.

Assorted Batiks
◆ Cut 250 squares $1^7/_8$" x $1^7/_8$", then cut in half diagonally for pinwheels.

Gold Batik
◆ Cut 3 strips $3^1/_4$" x fabric width, then cut into 26 squares $3^1/_4$" x $3^1/_4$", then cut in half diagonally twice for border #3.

◆ Cut 2 squares $2^7/_8$" x $2^7/_8$", then cut in half diagonally for border #3 corners.

Print
◆ Cut 2 strips $1^1/_4$" x $42^1/_2$" for the top and bottom borders #1.

◆ Cut 2 strips $1^1/_4$" x 44" for the side borders #1. (If your fabric is less than 44" without the selvages, cut one extra strip, cut it in half, and piece to the other strips end to end.)

PIECING AND PRESSING

Use $1/_4$" seam allowances. Press the direction the arrows indicate.

6" Nine-Patch Pinwheel Blocks

Pinwheels
You will need 5 pinwheels per block (125 total).

1 Stitch a $1^7/_8$" off-white triangle and a $1^7/_8$" batik triangle with right sides together. Press. Make 4 half-square triangle units for each pinwheel.

2 Stitch the 4 triangle units into a pinwheel. Press.

Press open.

Stitch half-square triangle unit.   Stitch units.

3 Stitch 5 pinwheels and 4 small alternate blocks together as shown. Press. Make 25 Nine-Patch Pinwheel blocks.

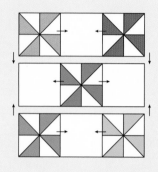

Stitch and press.

QUILT TOP ASSEMBLY

1 Lay out the Pinwheel blocks and large alternate blocks as shown in the diagram.

2 Stitch the blocks into rows. Press.

3 Stitch the rows together. Press. Your quilt top should measure $42^1/_2$" x $42^1/_2$".

Border #1

Depending on the width of the fabric you are using, it might be necessary to piece strips together end to end to get the needed length.

1 Trim 2 strips of the print fabric to 1 1/4" x 42 1/2" for the top and bottom. Stitch onto the top and bottom of the quilt top. Press.

2 Trim 2 strips to 1 1/4" x 44" for the sides. Stitch onto the sides of the quilt top. Press.

Border #2

1 Stitch the 5 3/4" off-white top and bottom borders onto the top and bottom of the quilt top. Press.

2 Stitch the side borders onto the sides. Press.

Border #3

1 Stitch a 3 1/4" off-white quarter-square triangle and a 3 1/4" gold batik quarter-square triangle with right sides together as shown. Press the exposed bias edges very carefully.

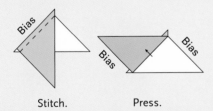

Stitch.   Press.

2 Stitch a 3 1/4" off-white quarter-square triangle to the unit as shown. Press.

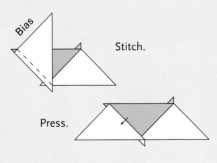

Press.

3 To make the outer border, continue adding triangles, beginning and ending with an off-white triangle. Make 4 borders, each with 27 off-white triangles and 26 batik triangles.

4 Stitch the top and bottom borders onto the quilt top. Press.

5 Stitch the side borders onto the quilt top. Press.

6 Stitch a 2 7/8" gold half-square triangle onto each corner. Press.

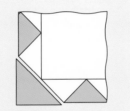

Stitch triangle to each corner.

QUILTING

Using the quilting designs on the pullout or drawing your own from the instructions beginning on page 17, find the center of the quilt and mark the feather wreath. Mark the feather flowers in the blocks and use the turned-feather border on the outside border. Note that there are two different corners. Using your see-through ruler, mark an approximately 3/4" grid using the pinwheels as guides. Layer, baste, and quilt. Bind following the instructions beginning on page 54.

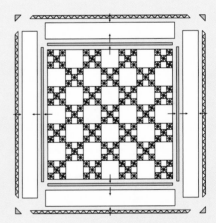

Quilt Construction

Quilting Designs

Bar Variation

This wallhanging is 30$\frac{1}{2}$" x 30$\frac{1}{2}$". Pieced by Alex Anderson and hand quilted by Elke Torgerson.

FABRIC REQUIREMENTS

Fabric amounts are based on a 42" fabric width.

Assorted blues and greens: $1/8$ yard each of 7 fabrics (2 lights, 2 mediums, 3 medium-darks) for pieced bars
Orange: $1/2$ yard for corners and bars
Red: $5/8$ yard for border
Backing: 1 yard
Batting: 35" x 35"
Binding: $1/3$ yard

CUTTING

For the bars, I used 7 fabrics and the piecing method below to obtain a random, scrappy look.

Assorted Blues and Greens
◆ Cut 1 strip 2" x fabric width of each color.
Orange
◆ Cut 2 rectangles $4 1/4$" x $18 1/2$".
◆ Cut 4 squares $6 1/2$" x $6 1/2$".
Red
◆ Cut 4 rectangles $6 1/2$" x $18 1/2$".

PIECING AND PRESSING

Use $1/4$" seam allowances. Press the direction the arrows indicate.

1 Alternating colors, stitch the 7 assorted blue and green strips together along the long side. Press.

Stitch.

2 Trim the selvages off one end, and cut into 6 units 4" wide.

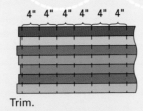

Trim.
Cut into units.

3 Stack and stitch the 6 units into one continuous row.

Stitch units into one continuous row.

4 Using your seam ripper, remove the stitching to create 3 sections, each with 12 rectangles. You will have a section of 6 rectangles left over.

NOTE: *Using this method to stitch and unstitch the sections creates the random placement of colors.*

5 Lay out the bars, alternating the 3 pieced bars with the 2 orange bars. Stitch the bars together. Press.

6 Stitch 2 of the red borders onto the sides of the quilt top. Press.

7 Stitch the 4 orange corner squares onto both ends of the 2 remaining red borders. Press.

Then stitch these borders onto the top and bottom of the quilt top. Press.

QUILTING

Using the quilting designs on the pullout, or drawing your own from the instructions beginning on page 17, trace the cable quilting design onto the orange bar strips, a diagonal grid onto the pieced bars, and the border feather onto the border. Layer, baste, quilt, and bind following the general instructions beginning on page 54.

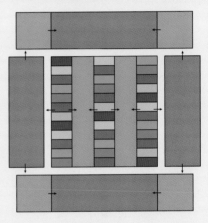

Quilt Construction

Quilting Designs

Diamond Variation

This wallhanging is 30¹/₂" x 30¹/₂". Pieced by Alex Anderson and hand quilted by Elke Torgerson.

FABRIC REQUIREMENTS

Fabric amounts are based on a 42" fabric width.

Yellow: $1/3$ yard each of four different yellows (1 light, 2 medium, and 1 dark)
Blue: $5/8$ yard
Backing: 1 yard
Batting: 35" x 35"
Binding: $1/3$ yard

CUTTING

Yellows

◆ Cut 1 square $9^7/8$" x $9^7/8$" from the lightest and the darkest yellows, then cut in half diagonally.

◆ Cut 2 squares $9^7/8$" x $9^7/8$" from the medium yellow, then cut in half diagonally.

◆ Cut 4 squares $6^1/2$" x $6^1/2$" from the remaining yellow.

Blue

◆ Cut 4 strips $6^1/2$" x $18^1/2$".

PIECING AND PRESSING

Use $1/4$" seam allowances. Press the direction the arrows indicate.

1 Lay out the yellow half-square triangles following the photograph for color placement. Stitch the triangles into squares.

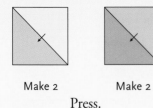

Make 2   Make 2
Press.

Stitch the triangles into squares.

2 Stitch the squares together. Press.

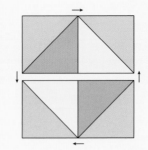

Stitch and press.

3 Stitch 2 of the blue borders onto the sides of the quilt top. Press.

4 Stitch the 4 yellow corner squares onto both ends of the 2 remaining blue borders. Press. Then stitch these borders onto the top and bottom of the quilt top. Press.

QUILTING

Using the quilting designs on the pullout, or drawing your own from the instructions beginning on page 17, mark the eight-pointed star and feathered wreath onto the center with hearts in the corners. Mark the cable border onto the borders. Layer, baste, quilt and bind following the general instructions beginning on page 54.

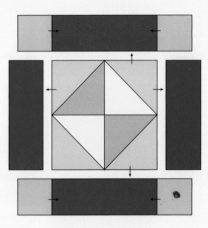

Quilt Construction

Quilting Designs

Sailboat

This wallhanging is 34$\frac{1}{2}$" x 34$\frac{1}{2}$" and is made up of four 8" Sailboat blocks.
Pieced by Alex Anderson and machine quilted by Paula Reid.

This quilt was fun and fast to make using only the existing fabrics in my stash. Notice that the sails use only a few inches of fabric.

FABRIC REQUIREMENTS

Fabric amounts are based on a 42" fabric width.

Assorted Blues: 10 scraps 3" x 3" each for sails

Assorted Reds: 4 scraps 3" x 10" each for hulls

White Print #1: ³/₈ yard for background

White Print #2: ¹/₈ yard for cornerstones

Blue: 1 yard for sashing and outer border

Red: ¹/₄ yard for inner border

Backing: 1 ¹/₈ yards

Batting: 38" x 38"

Binding: ¹/₃ yard

CUTTING

Assorted Blues

◆ Cut 10 squares 2⁷/₈" x 2⁷/₈", then cut in half diagonally for sails.

Assorted Reds

◆ Cut 4 rectangles 2¹/₂" x 9¹/₄" for hulls.

White Print #1

◆ Cut 2 strips 2⁷/₈" x fabric width, then cut into 16 squares 2⁷/₈" x 2⁷/₈". Cut in half diagonally for background.

◆ Cut 2 strips 2¹/₂" x fabric width, then cut into 4 squares 2¹/₂" x 2¹/₂" and 8 rectangles 2¹/₂" x 6¹/₂" for boat background.

White Print #2

◆ Cut 1 strip 2¹/₂" x fabric width, then cut into 9 squares 2¹/₂" x 2¹/₂" for cornerstones.

Blue

◆ Cut 3 strips 2¹/₂" x fabric width, then cut into 12 rectangles 2¹/₂" x 8¹/₂" for sashing.

◆ Cut 2 strips 5¹/₂" x 26" (they will be trimmed to size later) for the side outer borders.

◆ Cut 2 strips 5¹/₂" x 36" (they will be trimmed to size later) for the top and bottom outer borders.

Red

◆ Cut 2 strips 1¹/₂" x 24" (they will be trimmed to size later) for the side inner borders.

◆ Cut 2 strips 1¹/₂" x 26" (they will be trimmed to size later) for the top and bottom inner borders.

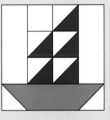

Sailboat Block

PIECING AND PRESSING

Use ¹/₄" seam allowances. Press the direction the arrows indicate.

1 Stitch a white print triangle and a blue triangle with right sides together. Press. Make 5 half-square triangle units.

Stitch half-square triangle unit.

2 Trim each end of the 2¹/₂" x 9¹/₄" rectangles at 45° as shown, to make the hulls.

Trim at 45°.

3 Stitch a white print triangle to each end of the hull. Press.

Stitch triangles to hull.

4 Stitch the block together as shown. Press. Make 4 blocks.

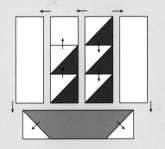

Stitch together.

QUILT TOP ASSEMBLY

1 Lay out the blocks, sashing, and cornerstones as shown. Stitch into horizontal rows. Press.

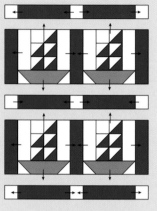

Stitch into rows.

2 Stitch the rows together. Press.

The top should measure 22 1/2" x 22 1/2". If it does, use the following instructions to attach the borders. If it doesn't, refer to page 54 to measure and adjust the borders to fit your quilt top.

Inner Border

1 Trim 2 red strips to 1 1/2" x 22 1/2". Stitch onto each side of the quilt top. Press.

2 Trim 2 strips to 1 1/2" x 24 1/2". Stitch onto the top and bottom. Press.

Outer Border

1 Trim 2 blue strips to 5 1/2" x 24 1/2". Stitch onto each side of the quilt top. Press.

2 Trim 2 strips to 5 1/2" x 34 1/2". Stitch onto the top and bottom. Press.

QUILTING

Mark a 2" diagonal grid in the blocks. Using the quilting designs on the pullout, mark the single cable in the inner border, and the dolphins, anchors and stars in the outer border. Add the rope curve. Layer, baste and quilt! Bind following the instructions beginning on page 54. Ahoy!

Quilt Construction

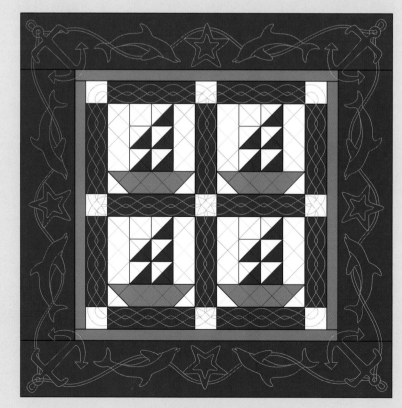

Quilting Designs

Rose of Sharon

This quilt is 83¼" x 83¼" and is made of nine Rose of Sharon blocks, thirty-six 5" Sawtooth Star blocks, twenty 5" alternate blocks, eight Three-Patch blocks, and an appliqué vine border.
Pieced, appliquéd, and quilted by Alex Anderson.

This quilt was inspired by a poem by Polly Chase Boydon from The Illustrated Treasury of Children's Literature ©*1955.*

Mud

Mud is very nice to feel
All squishy–squash
between the toes!
I'd rather wade in wiggly mud
Than smell a yellow rose.
Nobody else but the
rosebush knows
How nice mud feels
Between the toes.

FABRIC REQUIREMENTS

Fabric amounts are based on a 42" fabric width.

Off-white: 7 1/4 yards for background
Yellow: 2 1/4 yards total of assorted yellows for stars and flowers
Assorted Greens: 1 1/3 yards total for leaves and trumpets
Green: 3/4 yard for vine
Assorted Oranges: 1/2 yard total for flowers, flower centers, and grapes
Backing: 7 1/3 yards
Batting: 88" x 88"
Binding: 5/8 yard

CUTTING

Off-White

◆ Cut 2 lengthwise strips 10" x 66" for the border background (these will be trimmed to size later).

◆ Cut 2 lengthwise strips 10" x 85" for the border background (these will be trimmed to size later).

◆ Cut 5 strips 16" x fabric width, then cut into 9 squares 16" x 16" (these will be trimmed to size after the appliqué is completed).

◆ Cut 7 strips 1 3/4" x fabric width, then cut into 144 squares 1 3/4" x 1 3/4" for the stars.

◆ Cut 4 strips 3 3/4" x fabric width, then cut into 36 squares 3 3/4" x 3 3/4", then cut in half diagonally twice for the stars.

◆ Cut 3 strips 5 1/2" x fabric width, then cut into 20 squares 5 1/2" x 5 1/2" for the alternate blocks.

◆ Cut 3 strips 2 1/4" x fabric width, then cut into 16 squares 2 1/4" x 2 1/4" and 16 rectangles 2 1/4" x 4" for the Three-Patch blocks.

◆ Cut 2 strips 8 3/8" x fabric width, then cut into 8 squares 8 3/8" x 8 3/8", then cut in half diagonally twice for the pieced side triangles and pieced corner triangles.

◆ Cut 2 squares 4 3/8" x 4 3/8", then cut in half diagonally for the pieced corner triangles.

Yellow

◆ Cut 3 strips 3" x fabric width, then cut into 36 squares 3" x 3" for the stars.

◆ Cut 8 strips 2 1/8" x fabric width, then cut into 144 squares 2 1/8" x 2 1/8", then cut in half diagonally for the stars.

◆ Cut 2 strips 2 1/4" x fabric width, then cut into 24 squares 2 1/4" x 2 1/4" for the Three-Patch blocks.

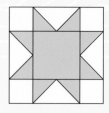

Sawtooth Star Block

PIECING AND PRESSING

Use 1/4" seam allowances. Press the direction the arrows indicate.

Sawtooth Star Blocks

1 Stitch a 2 1/8" yellow half-square triangle to each side of a 3 3/4" off-white quarter-square triangle as shown. Press. Make 4 per block.

Stitch triangles to make star points.

2 Stitch 2 star point units to a 3" yellow square as shown. Press. Stitch a 1 3/4" white square to each side of the remaining star point units. Press. Make 36 Stars.

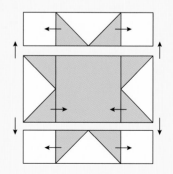

Stitch points to center square.

3 Lay out 4 Sawtooth Star blocks and 5 off-white 5" alternate blocks as shown.

4 Stitch the blocks into rows and press. Stitch the rows together. Press. Make 4 blocks.

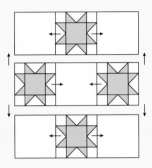

Stitch and press.

Pieced Side Triangles

1 Stitch together 3 yellow 2 1/4" squares, 2 off-white 2 1/4" squares, and 2 off-white 2 1/4" x 4" rectangles as shown to make a Three-Patch block. Trim to 5 1/2" square if needed. Press. Make 8 Three-Patch blocks.

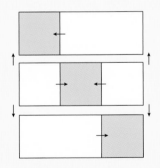

Stitch the Three-Patch block.

2 Stitch 2 Sawtooth Star blocks, one Three-Patch block, and 3 quarter-square triangles as shown. Press. Make 8 pieced side triangles.

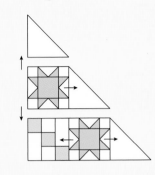

Stitch pieced side triangles.

Pieced Corner Triangles

Stitch 2 quarter-square triangles, a 4 3/8" half-square triangle, and a Sawtooth Star block as shown to make a pieced corner triangle. Press. Make 4.

Stitch pieced corner triangle.

APPLIQUÉ

Appliqué Preparation

Use your favorite appliqué preparation methods.

1 Prepare 17 yards of 1/4" bias vine. (I store mine on a toilet paper roll.)

2 Prepare 276 leaves.

3 Prepare 36 flowers for the wreaths and 9 triple-layered flowers for the wreath centers.

4 Prepare 32 trumpet flowers for the border vine.

5 Prepare 204 grapes 3/4" in size.

Rose of Sharon Block

Rose of Sharon Block

1 Press the 16" background square in half vertically, horizontally, and diagonally in both directions to mark placement lines.

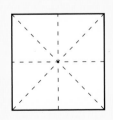

Fold placement lines.

2 Using a compass, draw a 10 1/4" circle in the center of the 16" square.

3 Center the vine sections on the circle and appliqué in place.

4 Find the center of the block, then appliqué the three layers and center of the triple flower into place.

5 Arrange the 4 flowers over the ends of the circle vine sections, then appliqué into place.

6 Arrange the 20 leaves around the wreath, then appliqué into place. Make 9 blocks.

7 Press the blocks wrong side up on a soft towel.

8 Trim each block to 15 1/2" x 15 1/2".

QUILT TOP ASSEMBLY

1 Lay out the blocks in a diagonal set referring to the diagram for block placement.

2 Stitch the blocks and the side pieced triangles into diagonal rows. Press.

3 Stitch all the rows together. Press.

4 Add the pieced corner triangles. Press.

Your quilt should measure 64 1/4" x 64 1/4". If it does, use the following instructions to add the borders. If it doesn't, refer to page 54 to measure and adjust the borders to fit your quilt top.

Border

The border is much easier to appliqué before it is attached to the quilt. Appliqué three quarters of each border, leaving the corners to be appliquéd once the border is stitched onto the quilt top.

1 Press the border pieces in half vertically and horizontally. Use these creases to help position and mark the feather border quilting design from the pullout. Use the photograph and quilting design to help with the placement of the appliqué pieces.

2 Appliqué the borders. Remember to leave enough unattached vine to turn the corners. You will cover the ends of each corner vine with a grape once the border is stitched onto the quilt top.

3 Trim the top and bottom borders to 64 1/4" and the side borders to 83 1/4".

4 Press the borders, wrong-side up, on a soft towel.

5 Stitch the top and bottom borders onto the quilt top. Press toward the border.

6 Stitch the side borders onto

the quilt top. Press toward the border.

7 Finish stitching the appliqué in the corners. Press.

QUILTING

Using the quilting designs on the pullout, or drawing your own from the instructions beginning on page 17, mark the feather design in the star blocks, and the feather border in the border. Mark an approximately 1" grid in the remaining background. Layer and baste. Quilt around the appliqué pieces and then on the marked lines. Do not quilt across the appliqué pieces. Bind following the instructions beginning on page 54.

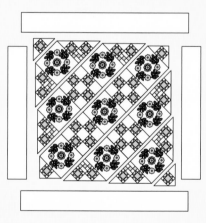

Quilt Construction (border appliqué not shown)

Quilting Designs (border appliqué not shown)

Leaf

Grape

Center Flower

Wreath Flower

Trumpet Flower

Trumpet Stem

Wreath Layout

The·Basics

STITCHING

Use a ¼" seam allowance and set the stitch length on your machine just long enough so that your seam ripper slides nicely in under the stitches.

BORDERS

If your quilt top measurements don't match the measurements given in the project instructions, follow the instructions below.

1 Cut the side border strips the length of your quilt top from top to bottom, by the border width given in the project instructions. Pin and sew to the sides of the quilt top. Press following the pressing arrows.

2 Measure your quilt top from side to side across the center, including the borders. Cut the top and bottom border strips this length. Pin and sew to the top and bottom of the quilt top. Press.

BATTING

For hand quilting, I recommend starting with a low-loft polyester batting. It makes the quilting stitch much easier to learn.

For machine quilting, I recommend that you use 100% cotton batting (prewash if necessary).

LAYERING

Place the backing *wrong* side up on your carpet or work surface. Keeping the fabric grain straight, smooth and stretch the backing taut and tape down. Layer the batting on top of the backing. Trim to the same size as the backing. Smooth the quilt top, right side up, onto the batting.

BASTING

For Hand Quilting

Baste in a grid pattern (about every 4") using large stitches through all three layers.

For Machine Quilting

Pin baste every 3" with safety pins. Pin evenly across the quilt, staying away from where the quilting stitches will be sewn.

QUILTING

Hand Quilting Stitches

To get started:

1 Put your basted quilt in a hoop or on a frame.

2 Put a small single knot in the thread. Insert the needle through the quilt top and batting (not into the backing) an inch away from where you want to start quilting and bring it up where you will start quilting. Gently pull on the thread, running your thumbnail over the knot to help pop the knot between the layers. This is called "burying" the knot.

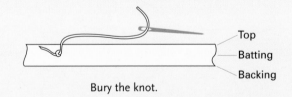

Top
Batting
Backing

Bury the knot.

3 The thimble indentations hold the blunt end of the needle, while your thumb on top and your hand underneath work together to create hills and valleys that the needle will then pass through to create the running stitch. Work from the center of the quilt to the outside edge to keep the layers smooth and avoid tucks.

4 When you come to the end of your thread, create another single knot and bury it between the three layers. Pull the remaining amount of thread up and carefully snip off the end.

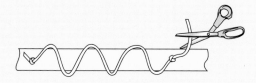

Bury the knot and cut the thread.

Machine Quilting

Machine quilting is an art form of its own. With practice, machine quilting can be a beautiful addition to your quilts.

To start machine quilting, stitch in the ditch or in a grid. Backtack at the beginning and end of each row. Starting in the center, stitch one row in each direction, both vertically and horizontally, to secure the three layers. Then work from the center out and quilt the remaining lines. Stitch in-the-ditch around the border seams and add quilting in the border.

BINDING

1 Trim the batting and backing even with the edges of the quilt top.

2 Cut 2$\frac{1}{4}$" x 42" strips. Trim them to the width of the quilt from side to side, plus 1" for trimming. If your quilt is over 42" wide, you will need to piece strips together to get the desired length. Sew the binding strips together with a diagonal seam. This will prevent a big lump in the binding.

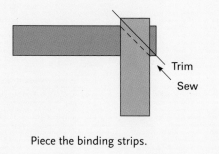

Piece the binding strips.

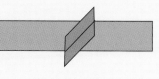

Trim the seams.

3 Fold and press lengthwise.

Fold and press.

4 On the top edge of the quilt, line up the raw edges of the binding with the raw edge of the quilt. Let the binding extend $\frac{1}{2}$" past the corners of the quilt. Sew using a $\frac{1}{4}$" seam allowance. Do this on the top and bottom edges of the quilt.

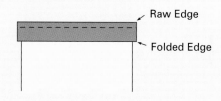

Attach the binding to the front of the quilt.

5 Turn the finished edge of the binding over the raw edge of the quilt and slipstitch the binding to the backing. Trim the ends even with the edge of the quilt.

6 Cut two 2$\frac{1}{2}$" x 42" strips. For the two remaining sides of the quilt, measure the length of the quilt from top to bottom. Trim the strips to this measurement plus $\frac{1}{2}$" for turning under. Sew the binding strips on, then fold over the end of the binding to create a finished edge before folding the binding to the back side. Slipstitch the binding to the backing.

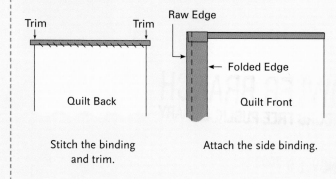

Stitch the binding and trim.

Attach the side binding.

About · The · Author

Alex Anderson's love affair with quiltmaking began in 1978, when she completed her Grandmother's Flower Garden quilt as part of her work toward a degree in art at San Francisco State University. Over the years her focus has rested upon understanding fabric relationships, and an intense appreciation of traditional quilting surface design and star quilts.

Alex currently hosts Home and Garden Television's quilt show *Simply Quilts*. Her quilts have been shown in magazines, including several articles specifically about her works.

Alex lives in Northern California with her husband, two children, two cats, one dog, one fish, and the challenges of suburban life. Visit her website at alexandersonquilts.com.

For more information write for a free catalog:
C&T Publishing, Inc.
P.O. Box 1456
Lafayette, CA 94549
(800) 284-1114
email: ctinfo@ctpub.com
website: www.ctpub.com

For quilting supplies:
Cotton Patch Mail Order
3405 Hall Lane, Dept. CTB
Lafayette, CA 94549
(800) 835-4418
(925) 283-7883
email: quiltusa@yahoo.com
website: www.quiltusa.com

Please Note:
Fabrics used in the quilts shown may not be currently available since fabric manufacturers keep most fabrics in print for only a short time.

Other books by
Alex Anderson: